WHO KNEW?
DISNEYLAND

WHO KNEW? DISNEYLAND

Little-known Facts About the Happiest Place on Earth

DAVID HOFFMAN

SHELTER HARBOR PRESS
NEW YORK

This revised edition published in 2017 by Shelter Harbor Press.

ISBN-13: 978-1-62795-103-6

Revised text copyright © 2017 by David Hoffman

Book design by Igor Satanovsky

Inside: **Shutterstock:** Olga Axyutina 106, 3DMAVR 179, Baldyrgan 133, Dicogm 73, Fun Way Illustration 1, Christopher Hall 46, 80, Ibrandify Gallery 35, Knumina Studios 50, Mureu 166, Ron and Joe 13, 16, 28, 31, 32, 55, 66, 85, 97, 139, 145, 154, 171, 183, John T Takai 5, Cory Thoman 151, Vector Illustration 19, Visual Generation 62; **Toon Vectors:** Ron Leishman 55, 190.

Cover: Shutterstock: Iraiu tr, Knumina Studios tm, Ron Leishman tl, Rtro br, Natalie Bakurina bm, Azuzi bl

SHELTER HARBOR PRESS
603 West 115th Street, Suite 163
New York, N.Y. 10025
Info@shelterharborpress.com

Printed and bound in China

10 9 8 7 6 5 4 3 2 1

DISCLAIMER

This book is a fun, enjoyable tribute to "the happiest place on earth" and is in no way authorized, endorsed, or sponsored by, nor is it affiliated with, the Disneyland Resort, the Walt Disney Company, or any of their subsidiaries, affiliates, or sponsors. All facts and figures were accurate, to the best of our knowledge, at the time it went to press. Disneyland, the Magic Kingdom, Mickey Mouse, Minnie Mouse, Donald Duck, the Mickey Mouse Club, Mouseketeers, Fantasyland, Tomorrowland, Adventureland, Frontierland, New Orleans Square, Toontown, Story-bookland, Disneyland Monorail, Disneyland Railroad, Mark Twain Riverboat, Sleeping Beauty Castle, It's a Small World, Mad Tea Party, Peter Pan's Flight, King Arthur's Carousel, Finding Nemo Submarine Voyage, Star Tours — The Adventure Continues, Space Mountain, Splash Mountain, the Matterhorn, The Many Adventures of Winnie the Pooh, Snow White's Scary Adventure, Tarzan's Tree-house, Jungle Cruise, Enchanted Tiki Room, Indiana Jones Adventure, Tom Sawyer Island, Pirates of the Caribbean, Haunted Mansion, Big Thunder Mountain Railroad, Dumbo the Flying Elephant, Great Moments with Mr. Lincoln, Club 33, Company D, Fantasy In the Sky, Remember… Dreams Come True, Main Street Electrical Parade, Audio-Animatronics, PeopleMover, Innoventions, Adventure thru Inner Space, and any other Disney character or Disneyland Resort ride, attraction, or locale that is mentioned in the book (but perhaps not mentioned on this page) are all registered trademarks and property of the Walt Disney Company, all rights reserved.

Whew.

According to public records, the official address of Disneyland is 1313 S. Harbor Boulevard. Because there were no buildings (and hence no existing addresses) in the area when the park was under construction, Walt was able to select any street number he wanted. It's been said that he went with 13 because the thirteenth letter of the alphabet is M, which would then make the address MM — for Mickey Mouse. However, 1313 was also the number that Disney artists had used as Donald Duck's address, 313 was Donald's license plate number, and the 13th (of July) was the Disneys' wedding anniversary, so it's also likely that Walt simply considered 13 to be his lucky number.

When Disneyland opened its gates on July 17, 1955, it had just 18 rides and attractions. Today there are more than 60 (with 12 of the original still in operation).

The average cost per guest on opening day was $2.37: $1 for admission, $0.25 for parking, and the rest for rides and souvenirs. According to the Consumer Price Index, that presently equals $21.47; however, the actual current cost will run closer to $196.

Disney management still refers to opening day as "Black Sunday." Temperatures were well over 100 degrees, drinking fountains were dry (thanks to a plumbers' strike), toilets clogged, food ran out, there was a gas leak in Fantasyland, and women's high heels sank into the asphalt on Main Street. To make it easier for female guests to get around, they were given a free pair of moccasins, because those were the only shoes Disneyland sold for adults.

WHO KNEW

Minutes prior to the official opening, there were areas of the park so lined with weeds that Walt instructed the landscapers to place signs bearing exotic, Latin-sounding species names next to them, to resemble an arboretum.

Mickey and Minnie and other walk-around characters were on-hand during the opening day, but because they did not roam the streets of the park regularly until the late 1950s, their costumes had to be borrowed from the Ice Capades, which had a Disney segment in their touring show.

In addition to the likes of Tomorrowland, Fantasyland and Adventureland, the park's original architectural drawings included a Land of Oz. At the time, Walt Disney Studios owned the rights to L. Frank Baum's books.

In the park's planning stage, Tom Sawyer Island was called Mickey Mouse Island and was home to the Mickey Mouse Club and the Mouseketeers. Walt soon changed his mind, in part because Tom Sawyer made more sense for Frontierland, but mostly to insure, should the park go belly up, that Mickey would not be associated with the failure. This was also the reasoning behind the decision to have Tinkerbell, not Mickey, introduce the Disneyland TV series every week.

The first person to utter the line, "I'm going to Disneyland" (and get paid to do so) was New York Giants quarterback Phil Simms, following his team's victory at Super Bowl XXI in 1987.

First names are featured on the name badges worn by all Disneyland (and Disney) employees, regardless of their position within the company (even the horses on Main Street have name tags). This practice dates back to 1962 and Walt's dislike of being called "Mr. Disney."

One of the employees of Disneyland in the 1960s was Steve Martin, who honed his talent for crafting balloon animals — a staple of his early standup act — while working at the Magic Shop. Other now-famous former Disneyland cast members include Michelle Pfeiffer (she played Alice in Wonderland in the Main Street Electrical Parade) as well as Kevin Costner and Pixar/Disney Animation CCO John Lasseter (he did duty as a skipper on the Jungle Cruise).

Former Secretary of State Henry Kissinger was such a fan of Disneyland that in the 1970s he would visit to get lost in the crowd and escape from the stress and pressure of his job. One day, for fun, he put on a uniform and sold popcorn from a cart. People gave him a second look, especially on hearing his distinctive voice and accent, but he still went the whole shift unrecognized.

The ground at the entrance to the park is red to simulate a red carpet, and to make every guest feel like a V.I.P.; on entering Main Street, the pavement becomes black, because black gets hot and "hot" keeps crowds moving — not just into the park, but directly into the stores.

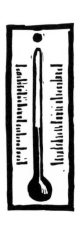

To encourage guests to buy sweatshirts and warm clothing, the Disney Clothiers, Ltd store is kept several degrees cooler than the other shops on Main Street.

WHO KNEW

Among the original stores on Main Street was the Hollywood Maxwell Corset Shop, also known as "The Wizard of Bras."

There is no elaborate system of tunnels connecting all of Disneyland underground; still, the park does have some interesting subterranean spaces, including one narrow walkway that runs below Tomorrowland (from beneath the former Innoventions Building — which now houses the Star Wars Launch Bay — to the area opposite the southern end of the Matterhorn). While it is occasionally used to get performers to and from the Terrace stage, its primary purpose is for trash removal and maintenance.

One fail-proof way to identify your location in the park: check out the garbage cans. While uniform in size and shape, they are painted in a different color in each of the different "lands."

Disneyland's New Orleans Square is several stories high, and as a result, the boarding area for Pirates of the Caribbean is on the equivalent of the third floor. What's underneath? The lower level of the attraction, along with offices, the main kitchen for this part of the park, and "the DEC" (the Disney Employee Cafeteria). The entrance to this area can be found to the immediate left of the Disneyland Railroad's New Orleans Square station, just before the restrooms.

Disneyland may be a world unto itself, but, technically it is part of the city of Anaheim, so park construction must adhere to municipal building codes. This can get interesting: special considerations had to be made for the Matterhorn because, at 147 feet, it exceeded the city's maximum height allowances; and local ordinances had to be amended for Submarine Voyage, given that land-locked Anaheim had no provisions on the books pertaining to the operation of underwater vessels within city limits.

The opening of Submarine Voyage in 1959, followed by the Matterhorn and the Monorail, inaugurated the E ticket. Up until that time, there had only been A, B, C, and D tickets. The last E-ticket ride added to Disneyland before the Park switched to the current single price admissions policy was Big Thunder Mountain Railroad, in 1979.

When Submarine Voyage was re-themed as Finding Nemo is 2007, Disney Imagineers wanted to insure that the intense colors of the attraction would not fade in the Southern California sun, so they pioneered a new technique which allowed them to "paint" the coral and rocked-in the lagoon with thirty tons of crushed recycled glass.

The topography surrounding Big Thunder Mountain Railroad was based on the thin, tall spires of rock found in abundance at Bryce Canyon National Park in Utah. A majority of the mining equipment visible while waiting in line or riding the attraction is authentic.

Disneyland's Matterhorn was the first roller coaster to use tubular steel instead of wood for its track, and therefore it was the first to allow loops, corkscrews, and extreme changes in direction.

The Matterhorn has two different tracks, and which one you ride is determined by which of the two lines you choose to wait in. Seasoned park-goers know that the right line (next to Alice in Wonderland, in Fantasyland) puts you on the slower track, where the ride last 30 seconds longer, while the left line (towards Tomorrowland) feeds into the faster track, which has one unexpected drop and tighter turns.

There is a makeshift, but regulation-size, half-court on which employees can play basketball inside the Matterhorn.

Disneyland's Matterhorn is a 1:100 scale replica of the real mountain located in the Swiss Alps.

Sleeping Beauty Castle rises only 72 feet above the moat (making it no larger than an average four-story building). To create the illusion of size, designers employed "forced perspective," a trick in which things are scaled smaller as they are built higher — thus making structures appear bigger, taller, and grander than they actually are. The same construction technique was used on the storefronts on Main Street, where from the ground floor to the third story, the scale shifts from 9/10ths to 7/8ths to 5/8ths actual size.

The story that one spire of Sleeping Beauty Castle remains purposely unpainted to visually represent Walt's theory that "Disneyland will never be completed as long as there is imagination left in the world" makes good copy, but it is not true. Rather, when the castle was refurbished in the 1990s, that spire was finished with a patina process that was expected to yield better results than the gold leafing previously used. It didn't — and ultimately, the ensuing dullness simply made the spire look like it had been forgotten.

The inspiration for Sleeping Beauty Castle came from Neuschwanstein Castle in Bavaria, Germany, which was built by Ludwig II in homage to opera composer Richard Wagner.

WHO KNEW

The most expensive souvenir sold at Disneyland is a miniature $37,500 solid crystal replica of Cinderella's Castle, set with more than 28,000 Swarovski crystals.

The brass (or golden) spike, visible in the ground as you exit Sleeping Beauty Castle and head into Fantasyland, is widely — although incorrectly — believed to have been placed there by Walt to designate the geographical center of the park. According to civil engineers, it is not a spike at all, but a cap or marker (one of several dozen in the park) used to accurately align land surveying equipment.

The vegetation that lines the moat around Sleeping Beauty Castle primarily consists of junipers because it is one of the few types of foliage that swans will not eat.

The swans in the moat are leased by the park, and there is always one male and one female.

There is a sizable colony of feral cats in and around Disneyland, although park-goers do not usually see them due to their nocturnal nature. The grounds crews leave them alone, thanks to a devoted following (including 50K Instagram followers) but primarily because they (and how ironic is this?) help to keep the rodent population in check.

In designing, constructing, adding the final touches to, or upgrading an attraction, Disney artists often pay homage to the Mouse by subtly incorporating a silhouette of Mickey into their work. Most commonly, this is a graphic interpretation of his face, and uses three circles to represent his round head and two round ears. Known as a "Hidden Mickey," locating and identifying these inside jokes has become a popular pastime for die-hard Disney fans, and today, there are dozens throughout the park.

One of the first Hidden Mickeys was the model of the giant water molecule in the old Adventure Thru Inner Space attraction, where two small hydrogen atoms were positioned atop a single larger oxygen atom, forming not only H_2O, but a representation of the familiar Mickey face.

Adventure Thru Inner Space, the popular Tomorrowland attraction which (from 1967 to 1985) took passengers on a journey into the depths of an atom, was so dark inside that amorous park-goers took to using it as a place to get intimate – and cast members took to calling it "Adventure Thru Intercourse."

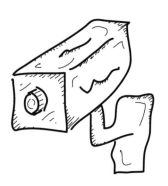

Despite the security systems now installed inside all of Disneyland's attractions (and the monitors being watched by park employees hidden from view), couples will still try to have sex while on the "dark rides" (such as Pirates of the Caribbean or It's a Small World), apparently not realizing that the cameras are infrared and can pick up their every move. On occasion they are stopped with a warning over the loud-speaker; other times, as they exit, they are met with applause from knowing cast members.

While cremated remains are on the list of items not permitted to be brought into the park, one recent problem facing Disneyland security has been guests smuggling in the ashes of their loved ones, with the intent of spreading them while on a favorite attraction. This recurs enough that ride operators are now instructed on how to handle the incident and the maintenance department has special vacuums with HEPA filters to tackle the clean-up.

Although the majority of the officers are dressed in plain clothes and go unnoticed, Disneyland's security force has more members than the City of Anaheim has police.

WHO KNEW

The all-time most popular Disneyland souvenir is a pair of personalized Mickey Mouse ears. Over eighty-four million have been purchased since opening day; enough to adorn every child in America under eighteen.

WHO KNEW

While the embroidery is free, the Mad Hatter and other shops that sell Mickey Mouse ears will not allow guests to have them adorned with the name of a famous person, corporation, sports team, or personal business. This does not stop guests from getting creative; one requested that "Vincent" be written on his, then after it was handed back to him, he tore off one of the ears.

Savvy bargain shoppers know that the best place to buy Disneyland merchandise isn't in the park, but a few miles east of it, at Company D — Team Center. You have to be a cast member (or lucky enough to score a voucher from one) to get in, and the selection can be hit or miss, but the discounts are always deep. The Property Control area is particularly worth a look: theatrical costumes as well as park furniture and one-of-a-kind set pieces can be among the items up for sale.

One item not sold at Disneyland is gum. Walt did not want his guests to constantly be stepping in it or picking it off their shoes, a pet peeve he had with other amusement parks.

In the early 1960s, a supplier to the Casa de Fritos Mexican restaurant suggested that instead of the kitchen throwing out any leftover tortillas, they should cut them up, fry them, add some basic seasoning — and serve them. The new menu item proved to be such a hit that parent company Frito-Lay packaged it as a snack and rolled it out nationwide, under the name Doritos.

The highly regarded, hand-dipped corn dog sold from the Little Red Wagon parked on Main Street (food critic Jonathan Gold of *The Los Angeles Times* has said it's the best he's ever eaten) comes served with a choice of sliced apples or a small bag of chips. But what many guests in line don't know is that they can also opt for neither "side" — and shave at least 25 percent off the price.

WHO KNEW

What gives the turkey legs sold at Disneyland their unique taste (and pink color) is that they are injected with a curing brine (with includes a special curing salt) and then they are smoked. It's no surprise that fans of these drumsticks say they taste like ham; this is the same cooking technique that is used to make wet cured ham.

Studies show that during prime meal hours, when the self-serve food operations are at their busiest, the lines on the left side tend to be shorter.

Scentertainment refers to the enhancement of the Disneyland experience by incorporating smells into various park areas and attractions, be it the aroma of chocolate, caramel apple, and waffle cone outside the Candy Palace on Main Street or the musky odor that hits you as you descend into the Pirates of the Caribbean.

Any attraction-specific smell (such as that of honey in The Many Adventures of Winnie the Pooh) is created when a pound of small translucent beads is loaded into a canon-like device called a Smellitzer, and air is shot through them, thereby releasing the scent. The Smellitzer also contains a micro-fan, which clears the air of the current scent before it releases the next one.

Many days at Disneyland begin with a "rope drop" that lets everyone in at once. The rope is positioned at the northern end of Main Street, where the shopping district ends. However, if your first stop is either Fanstasyland or Tomorrowland, instead of gathering there with the masses, consider slipping into any one of the already-opened shops on the east side of the street. Work your way through the shops — they're all connected — until you reach the side exit in the far back. This will not only put you even with the front of the Main Street crowd, but (once the ropes drop) a valuable few steps ahead of them.

Only twice in the park's history has Disneyland chosen not to open and then remained closed for the entire day: on Saturday, November 23, 1963 (the national day of mourning following the assassination of John F. Kennedy) and on September 11, 2001 (in response to the four terrorist attacks on the U.S.).

Among the free perks at Disneyland that are yours (or your kids) for the asking: a seat at the front of Monorail, a ride in the wheelhouse of the Mark Twain Riverboat, a Jungle Cruise Map (so you can follow your progress as you explore the jungle rivers of the world) and a roster of the names of each of the horses on King Arthur's Carousel (that list is available at City Hall).

Anyone, not just cast members, can wake up José the Macaw in the Enchanted Tiki Room. Simply ask a cast member as you enter, while the audience is being seated.

WHO KNEW

WHO KNEW

In the mid-1950s and continuing through the 1960s, animation cels, which can now command four and five figures, were considered fun to look at, but worthless, so thousands of original scenes from the early Disney films were sold at the park as souvenirs — for a buck each.

While the idea of Main Street was inspired by Walt's childhood hometown of Marceline, Missouri, chief designer Harper Goff grew up in Fort Collins, Colorado, so much of the architectural style is based on that city — in particular City Hall, which was modeled after the Fort Collins County Courthouse.

For the first year Disneyland was in operation, the Main Street Penny Arcade included a shooting gallery that used real guns — live ammunition .22-caliber rifles.

Tom Sawyer Island was originally stocked with catfish and provided poles for fishing, but the practice was discontinued when days-old catch, often having been abandoned in guest storage lockers, started to cause a stink.

Among the items that have turned up in the Disneyland Lost and Found are false teeth, wigs and toupees, a prosthetic limb, a glass eye, a waterbed, and a canary. On any given summer day, 210 pairs of sunglasses go missing.

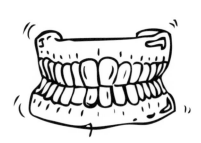

To avoid the lines at any popular attraction that does not offer a Fastpass, instead of heading there first, save it for last. It is park practice that unless an attraction plans to shut down early (cast members on the attraction will know if this is the case), anyone in line at the time of closing will be able to remain in line until they are able to board and ride.

The water tower adjacent to Frontierland is active and fully functional — and it is the source of power for the steam trains on the Disneyland Railroad.

The four original locomotives on the Disneyland Railroad were named after four executives of the Santa Fe Railroad: C.K. Holiday, E.P. Ripley, Ernest S. Marsh and Fred Gurley. Walt, a train buff, always had a soft spot for the Santa Fe, as it ran through his Missouri hometown.

The Town Square flag pole is recycled from a lamp post that once stood on Wilshire Boulevard in Los Angeles, and was purchased from the city for five dollars, after the fixture was knocked over in a car accident.

In the 1950s, Town Square included a store-front for a real estate company that was more than just show. Inside, licensed agents promoted suburban developments in Orange Country and sold land in Apple Valley, a (then) largely undeveloped area 80 miles northeast of Anaheim.

The baby in the vintage, framed photo that hangs on the wall of The Baby Care Center is Walt Disney.

As of 2017, there have been four babies born at Disneyland; all have been girls.

The two cannons in Town Square date back to the nineteenth century, and were originally built for and used by the French Army.

The gas streetlamps on Main Street are over 150 years old and were bought as scrap, for as little as three cents a pound, from St. Louis, Baltimore, and Philadelphia, which had no further use for them. It proved to be a good deal on several levels: in December 1982, the park had to be evacuated due to a power outage, and the gas lamps lit the way.

Each light in Disneyland is replaced when it has reached 80 percent of its anticipated life rather than when it fails.

Disneyland currently employs (full-time) an average of 54 electricians, 150 landscape gardeners, and 50 scuba divers.

The tracks running down Main Street are greased each morning with vegetable oil, so the streetcars can round corners safely, efficiently, and quietly.

WHO KNEW

There are no sharp 90-degree turns in the Main Street sidewalks. Walt felt that they would give the park a certain urban coldness, so to guarantee that Disneyland maintained its small town sense of warmth, all of the curbs were constructed using curves instead of corners.

The horses pulling streetcars on Main Street have a polyurethane coating on their shoes, partly because it gives them better traction, but mainly to heighten the clip-clop sound they make as they walk.

WHO KNEW

The tiny pieces embedded into the pavement of Main Street (often mistaken for discarded pieces of chewing gum) are sensors, that guide parade floats and ensure they hit their marks.

Though not open to the public, there is a 600-square-foot apartment over the Main Street Fire Station, where Walt would occasionally stay when he visited the park. It is still used today by visiting executives, the Disney family, and for small, private meetings.

The names painted on the second-story windows along Main Street are those of people who played a key role in Disneyland, the Walt Disney Company, or Disney's life. This was Walt's way of thanking, and permanently honoring, those who helped him realize his vision.

Names of Disneylanders who created, and continued to develop, the park's attractions can be found painted on the signs, buildings, boxes, trunks, and barrels incorporated into the design of various rides and lands, from the tombstones at the Haunted Mansion to the stacks of crates next to the Jungle Cruise.

"Benjamin Silverstein, M.D.," the name that appears on the Main Street door with a mezuzah next to it, was not a real person; rather, the façade was created so that there would be a fitting place for the park to put up Hanukkah decorations.

The depiction of Walt in the bronze "Partners" statue at the end of Main Street shows him wearing a tiepin with a stylized "STR" logo — the emblem for Smoke Tree Ranch in Palm Springs, California, a favorite vacation destination of his.

Designers modeling the Audio-Animatronic Abe to be used in Great Moments With Mr. Lincoln inadvertently discovered that when the rubber mold of the head was turned inside out, the President's eyes would appear to follow them wherever they went. The effect was creepy...so creepy that they incorporated this technique into the Haunted Mansion and cast the two busts found at the end of the hallway (as you exit the elevator) from molds that had been deliberately inverted.

WHO KNEW

The dancing ghosts in the ballroom of the Haunted Mansion are created through the use of an old magician's trick: the actual robots and mannequins going through the motions are concealed one story above, but are lit in a way that their ghostly likenesses are reflected in the glass in front of you.

The PeopleMover track system used to transport guests in the Haunted Mansion without relying on wheeled carriages was inspired by a conveyor belt (which was designed to safely lift and transport hot metal ingots) that Walt had seen on a visit to the Ford Motor Company plant.

WHO KNEW

The hardest task facing the maintenance crew assigned to clean the Haunted Mansion is keeping it looking dirty enough, so they regularly haul in cobwebs and five-pound bags of dust, which they then scatter around with a device similar to a fertilizer spreader.

The voice and face of the fallen bust in the Haunted Mansion belongs to Thurl Ravenscroft, who is not only the narrator of the Disneyland Railroad, but was (until his death in 2005) the voice of Tony the Tiger.

Among the more unique opportunities ever offered by the park was the chance to have a personalized tombstone placed in the graveyard at the Haunted Mansion. It sold at auction for $37,400; the proceeds went to charity.

To give the grounds outside the Haunted Mansion a sense of decay, particular varieties of heucheras, ajugas, and ipomoeas were selected by the landscape architects for their washed-out brown and dark green hues. If they were simply replaced with more vibrantly-colored red, purple, and pink varieties of the same plants, the gardens would then be beautiful.

It takes 10,000 flowers to complete the Mickey Mouse portrait at the park entrance. To create it, the gardeners install fiberglass header board into the soil to form the ears, eyes, nose, mouth, and cheeks. They then plant annuals of a designated color into each of the specific segments, much like painting by numbers.

Many of the plants in and around Tomorrowland are edible, to emphasize a future where gardens do double duty as food sources. This is most noticeable in the bushes along the walkways, which are planted with lettuce, kale, rhubarb, and an assortment of herbs.

Hedges throughout the park are treated with growth-retarding hormones to limit the need for pruning. Olive trees are also sprayed to prevent their fruit from maturing and falling, making it easier for maintenance to keep the sidewalks clean.

The names of virtually every plant and tree in the park are kept on file at City Hall. The records are open to any guest interested in knowing more about the landscaping they have seen.

While Tarzan's Treehouse (formerly the Swiss Family Robinson Treehouse) has been given the species name Disney-odendron, it was modeled after a real tree — a Moreton Bay Fig — that still stands less than two miles north of the park, in front of the house at 410 N. West Street in Anaheim.

The original Disneyland Bandstand was replaced by the bigger Plaza Gardens Dance Pavilion in 1956. But while it may be gone, it is not forgotten. The classic white gazebo (and piece of Opening Day history) was saved from the wrecking ball and now sits at Roger's Gardens (a nursery in nearby Corona del Mar, California) where it plays host to Santa every December.

Building Disneyland had used up all of Walt's capital, so in a quest to find a way to develop and test his latest ideas but with someone else footing the bill, it hit him to contact major corporations and offer to create attractions for them for the 1964 World's Fair. Among his clients were General Motors, General Electric, Ford, and Pepsi-Cola, and among the results was It's A Small World.

During peak season, when the park is open 16 hours a day, the It's a Small World theme song plays an average of 1,200 times.

According to the International Museum of Carousel Art, there is no difference between a carousel and a merry-go-round. While it is common that one-third of the animals on both are stationery, what sets Disneyland's King Arthur's Carousel apart is that it has been modified so that not only do all of the animals move, but all of the animals are horses and all of the horses are jumpers.

In the beginning, only one of the horses on King Arthur's Carousel was white. It proved so popular that all of the horses are now white, yet all are detailed differently.

A lesser-known spot from which to watch the nightly fireworks display is by the planters that surround King Arthur's Carousel. Not only does the edge of them provide a rare place to sit, but if Tinkerbell is part of the show, her flight path is directly over you.

In Peter Pan's Flight, as pirate ships escort park visitors through the window of the Darling children's bedroom, over London, and on to Neverland, observant guests will notice a set of blocks, whose letters spell out D-I-S-N-E-Y from the bottom up.

While experimenting with methods to make the miniature church roof in the Storybook Land Canal Boat Ride appear realistically old and weathered, a designer discovered that urine has an extremely corrosive effect on metal. So...

WHO KNEW

The Dumbo ride was first conceived as "Pink Elephants on Parade" and was to consist of all pink elephants, like the ones Dumbo envisions in his nightmare in the movie. Walt changed his mind, however, when he realized that it might look like he was encouraging kids to drink alcohol.

When President Harry Truman — a Democrat — visited Disneyland in 1957, he refused to ride on Dumbo, as he did not wish to be photographed with a giant elephant, the symbol of the Republican Party.

The decision to make the apple held by the Wicked Queen in Snow White's Scary Adventure a hologram was not based on a desire to employ the latest technology; it was motivated by the fact that for years the original 3-D apple was the park prop most frequently stolen by guests seeking souvenirs.

Initially, the storybook rides were designed so that guests could experience the attraction from the main character's point of view — so guests on Snow White's Scary Adventure, for example, WERE Snow White. But for years, nobody got it, and guests would regularly ask where Snow White — or Peter Pan or Alice in Wonderland — was. This was the main reason that Fantasyland was completely overhauled in 1983, and why today namesake characters are featured in their own rides.

Despite long-standing rumors, the 18 teacups on the Mad Tea Party are designed to spin at the same speed. That said, the key to making any cup go their fastest is for all riders to lean towards the center and for riders to alternate who turns the wheel. If more than two people do so at once, hands get in each other's way, and that will slow you down.

Mad Tea Party is the attraction most responsible for causing park guests to lose their lunch. Cast members refer to this as either a "Code V" or a "Protein Spill," and to clean up the mess, they cover it with "Barf Dust," a green, kitty litter-like substance that soaks up the mishap and enables it to be swept up easily.

Walt had the idea for Space Mountain in the 1960s but the technology was not available for its creation until a decade later.

Space Mountain had to be sunk nearly 20 feet into the ground when it was built so that it would be in proper proportion to Sleeping Beauty Castle and the Matterhorn.

WHO KNEW

The soundtrack you hear while riding Space Mountain is performed by Dick Dale, "King of the Surf Guitar."

Even at its fastest, Space Mountain never goes more than 30.3 mph.

The terminal announcement that plays in the waiting area leading into Star Tours — the Adventure Continues twice pays tribute to *Star Wars* director George Lucas: in a page for departing passenger Egroeg Sacul (Egroeg Sacul is George Lucas spelled backwards) and in an announcement that a landspeeder with the license plate THX1138 is parked in a no-hover zone. (*THX 1138* was Lucas' first film).

Disneyland has numerous attractions based on movies, and numerous movies have been based on Disneyland attractions, yet in all these years, only three feature films have ever been filmed on location at the park: *Forty Pounds of Trouble*, *That Thing You Do,* and *Saving Mr Banks*.

WHO REVIEW

The Submarine Voyage was comprised of eight vessels, which inadvertently made Walt the commander of the world's eighth-largest submarine fleet — a fact that caught the attention of — Soviet Premier Nikita Khrushchev. Ultimately, Khrushchev's trip to Disneyland to see them in 1959 was canceled by the U.S. State Department, over concerns that security was not adequate.

In the mid-1960s, when the novelty of the Submarine Voyage started to diminish, Disneyland executives attempted to revitalize it by stocking the lagoon with live "mermaids" in bikini tops. The gimmick did not last long: young male guests began jumping in (and swimming out) to have their photos taken with the maidens and several of the performers reportedly became ill from the chemicals in the water.

WHO KNEW

When the Disneyland Monorail opened in 1959 it was the first daily operating monorail in the Western hemisphere, and the first anywhere to cross a public street.

The first passenger to officially ride the Monorail was then Vice-President Richard Nixon and his family. This also marked — unbeknownst to Nixon, the Secret Service, and the press — the first time that the futuristic vehicle had made it all the way around the park without incident. In the days (hours!) leading up to the ribbon-cutting ceremony, every time the engineers had sent the Monorail around its track for a test run, it had caught on fire.

The "on time" rate of the Monorail is impressive: 99.9 percent. But expect to wait an average of 20 minutes if it (or any other attraction) needs to be restarted due to computer and safety protocols.

The transports used in the Indiana Jones Adventure do not travel at greater speeds than the vehicles on other attractions in the park, rather, thanks to a motion simulator that is part of their base, they just feel like they do. As a result, guests get the impression that they are moving at 65 mph, when in reality they are never going faster than 22 mph.

While most Audio-Animatronics of humans are mechanical forms that are ultimately, like mannequins, dressed in costume, the Indiana Jones figure was molded fully clothed, entirely out of rubber. Apparently, Audio-Animatronics are prone to leaking. The appeal of rubber versus a traditional cloth wardrobe which would need to be removed, washed, laundered, pressed, and replaced, is that it can be cleaned with a simple scrubbing,

When designer Harriet Burns was looking for the perfect material to use to make the "skin" for the birds in the Enchanted Tiki Room, she had to look no further than her boss: in a meeting, she noticed the cashmere sweater Walt was wearing moved at the elbows exactly the way that she needed.

The Enchanted Tiki Room is the only attraction in the park with its own restrooms. This is because it was initially planned as a restaurant with a dinner show, but the Audio-Animatronic part turned out to be so spectacular and well-received that the dining concept was scrapped before opening.

In Fantasyland, both the giant mushroom (on which the over-sized *Alice in Wonderland* storybook is perched) and the lighthouse (found near the Storybook Land Canal Boats) are artifacts from the park's earliest days — the two were built and used as ticket booths in a time when guests paid separately to ride each attraction.

Walt was willing to take risks, and as a result, not every Disneyland attraction was a big success. The shortest-lived one was the Mickey Mouse Club Circus, which featured live animal acts. However, most guests did not come to the park to see trained elephants (they came to see Mickey Mouse) so in less than two months of its November 1955 opening, the circus had folded up its tent and was gone.

According to early drawings, Adventureland was to be on the east side of the park, next to Tomorrowland. The location was changed when it was discovered that there was a pre-existing grove of eucalyptus trees on the west side of the property, which designers felt would work well with the exotic Polynesian motif that they were planning.

WHO KNEW

Walt's original park plan incorporated using a number of the orange trees on the property, so he tagged the ones he wanted to keep with red ribbons and marked the ones he wanted removed with green ribbons. Unfortunately, the bulldozer operator was color-blind, so, after he was done, none of the trees were left standing.

Collection mailboxes remain scattered throughout Disneyland, and while fully functional, they are also a reminder of a time when guests sent postcards instead of texts or tweets.

Splash Mountain has earned the nickname "Flash Mountain" thanks to those uninhibited female park-goers who have taken to lifting up their tops and exposing their breasts to the cameras snapping souvenir photos at the final waterfall. While any off-color images are supposed to be deleted by Disneyland employees, they often get saved, and many are now circulating on the internet.
Unzip-a-dee-doo-dah!

The final plunge of Splash Mountain sends guests 45 mph down a 52-foot drop, at a 47-degree angle — making it the fastest ride in the park.

The water in the Jungle Cruise is tinted (sometimes brown, sometimes bluish-green), not only to make the river look more real, but so that the bottom — which is only three feet deep in parts — cannot be seen.

When the Jungle Cruise opened it was based on *True Life Adventures*, Disney's popular series of nature documentaries, and was designed as a realistic journey along the rivers of Asia, Africa and South America. From the start, the tour was narrated by a Skipper, but his spiel was, in the spirit of the films, fact-filled and straightforward. The current version — and its plethora of bad puns — did not follow until some years later, when more comic elements were incorporated into the ride.

Walt's initial plan for the Jungle Cruise was that it would be inhabited by real hippos and elephants until the practicality of working with live animals — particularly in such a tiny area — caught up with him. Beyond worrying that wildlife, afraid of humans, might spend the day hiding or sleeping and out of sight of the guests came the realization that animals need to be fed, and animals who eat tend to leave a trail behind them.

The boats on the Jungle Cruise were modeled after the boat in *The African Queen,* starring Humphrey Bogart and Katharine Hepburn.

WHO KNEW

The Mark Twain Riverboat is a genuine
paddle wheeler, yet while it runs on steam,
it does so without needing a captain to
navigate it — thanks to a carefully hidden,
underwater guidance track.

WHO KNEW

The sailing ship *Columbia* is a full-scale replica of the first American vessel to sail around the world, but because those original plans were hard to come by, it was configured primarily using a set of very similar plans — those of the *HMS Bounty*, of *Mutiny on the Bounty* fame.

The underground, inter-terminal train that began operating at George Bush Inter-continental Airport in Houston, Texas in 1981 replicated the exact mechanical design of the former Tomorrowland PeopleMover and is the only transportation system outside of a Disney park that has been built by the Walt Disney Company.

A two-car unit from the Tomorrowland PeopleMover sold at a 2015 Los Angeles auction for $471,500, the highest price paid to date for a single piece of Disneyland memorabilia.

If you ring the doorbell at the Toontown firehouse, a Dalmatian puppy will appear in a second floor window.

The passport sitting in the glass case along the back wall of Mickey's house in Toontown is stamped with the names of five places (Anaheim, Orlando, Hong Kong, Paris, and Tokyo), each a city where a Disney park is located. The date of the stamp is the same as the date that the property officially opened.

Among the books lining the shelves of
Minnie's house is one in the kitchen that's
entitled "Elvis. What Happened?"

The trees lining the hills behind Minnie's house form the letters WDI — an homage to Walt Disney Imagineering.

Wayne Allwine, the actor who provided the voice for Mickey Mouse for 32 years (until his death in 2009), and Russi Taylor, the voice of Minnie Mouse since 1986, were husband and wife in real life. They met on the job.

According to the employee manuals from 1955 to 2000, male workers at Disneyland were not permitted to have facial hair. Which means that Walt — who wore a moustache — would not have been allowed to work at his own park.

Cast members hired to portray characters have to go through autograph training, so that signatures are consistent throughout the park (as well as from park to park). This also means that any autograph gotten at Disneyland today will look the same as one that was collected decades ago.

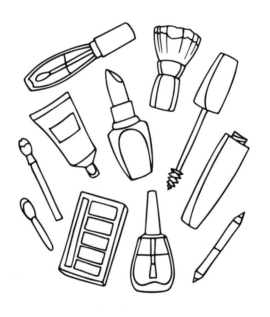

The cosmetics line used by all Disney
Princesses is Ben Nye Makeup.

If guests look beyond the fantasy, Disneyland does its best to see that they don't see anything at all. Hence, the oh-so-real utilitarian parts of the park — walls, fences, doors, units that house equipment, any concrete — are all painted in colors known internally as "Go Away Green" or "No See-um Gray" — shades that blend well with the landscape and are meant to make things go unnoticed.

The door front at 33 Royal Street in New Orleans Square (yes, the one painted No See-um Gray) with handsome Art Nouveau detailing and the number etched into the transom window above it, is not just another example of the park's attention to detail, but marks the (new) entrance to the members-only dining room known as Club 33. Inspired by the numerous companies who offered restricted-access lounges to VIPs visiting their pavilions at the 1964 World's Fair, Walt wanted a place in Disneyland where he could entertain investors and business associates.

When first constructed, one of Club 33's dining areas had microphones installed in an overhead chandelier. It is rumored that this set-up was Richard Nixon's idea, so that Walt could eavesdrop on guests. Not true. The plan behind the hidden listening devices was to allow actors (also unseen) to entertain diners by conversing with them in the guise of the Audio-Animatronic critters perched throughout that room. Today, one of these figures — a California turkey vulture — has been restored and can be found in the club's main foyer.

Membership in Club 33 is a mix of individuals and businesses, and caps off around 500. The limit is due to the capacity of the restaurant, not snobbery or exclusivity.

On average, Club 33 has a ten-year waiting list (at times, it has been as long as 14 years) that allows for 1,000 people. Although it, too, is often full.

At last report, members were paying $25,000 to join Club 33, plus almost $10,000 in annual dues.

It has often been reported that Club 33 got its numerical name from its address, and that the address itself was required in order for Disneyland to get the club a liquor license. But this theory is unlikely, since neither streets nor individual addresses inside the park are assigned (let alone recognized) by the United States Postal Service.

So why the "33' in Club 33? Many suspect that it is because the number turned sideways reads "MM'" (for Mickey Mouse) and/or looks like mouse ears. Another popular explanation points out that there were 33 original park sponsors and lessees whose belief and support helped turn Walt's dream of Disneyland into reality, and it was a tip of the hat to them.

The tapping sound coming from the Depot at the Disneyland Railroad station in New Orleans Square is a line from Walt's opening day speech ("To all who come to this happy place, welcome…") in a variant of Morse Code. However, early on in the park's history, the designers used any number of messages, and often, for fun, they would make them off-color comments — until Walt happened to mention that his wife Lillian had been a telegraph operator and could decipher Morse Code.

Some of the railings surrounding the second-floor balconies of New Orleans Square that are visible to guests, yet not accessible to them, are made of rubber instead of cast iron, as rubber will not rust and stands a better chance of weathering the elements.

The huge box office success of *Mary Poppins* provided a wealth of revenue for the Walt Disney Studios — and the funds that Walt needed to build New Orleans Square and Pirates of the Caribbean.

Pirates of the Caribbean was initially conceived as a standard wax museum, filled with pirate figures in staged settings. But working on four attractions for the New York World's Fair — including the development of the first human Audio-Animatronic (Abraham Lincoln) and an efficient way to move large groups of people through an experience (the use of boats in It's a Small World) — gave Walt and his designers the idea and the know-how to forego that notion and to make Pirates of the Caribbean a totally immersive environment.

When the Pirates of the Caribbean opened in 1967, the fake skeletons available to the Disney designers were unconvincing and looked like tacky Halloween decorations, so real specimens, which had previously been used for research, were purchased from UCLA's Medical Center. They've since been replaced.

By request of the Anaheim Fire Department, the Pirates of the Caribbean is equipped with a system that, in the event of an actual fire, automatically shuts down the authentic "burning town" effect found at the end of the ride, so that the City can pinpoint the real blaze and not waste time battling artificial flames.

Pirates of the Caribbean was the first attraction designed with so much happening simultaneously that it was impossible to see, hear, and experience everything in one pass. As a result, it revolutionized Disneyland by guaranteeing what has become the holy grail of the amusement park industry: the return visit.

Most guests leave the park only having understood the first line ("Yo ho, yo ho, a pirate's life for me") of the Pirates of the Caribbean theme song. Although hard to decipher, the rest of the verse goes as follows:
"We pillage, we plunder, we rifle, and loot
Drink up, me 'earties, yo ho
We kidnap and ravage and don't give a hoot
Drink up me 'earties, yo ho."

More Disneyland guests have ridden the Pirates of the Caribbean ride than any other attraction…ANYWHERE.

He's Mickey Mouse to you and me, but in Iran, he's known as Mickey Moosh; in Iceland, Mikki Mus; in Italy, Topolino; and in Sweden, Musse Pigg.

WHO KNEW

Disneyland greeted its one-millionth guest after less than eight weeks of operation.

It was a combination of the letters he got from kids (who wanted to visit the place where Mickey Mouse lived), his frustration that no city park offered equipment that parents could (comfortably) ride on along with their children, and his visit to The Henry Ford (a living history museum in Michigan) that fed Walt's plan to create a "land" where families could spend the day together.

The original site Walt had his eye on was the six-acre tract across from his studios in Burbank, California (now the location of the hat-shaped Walt Disney Feature Animation Building), but as his team came up with more and more ideas, his Mickey Mouse Park evolved into Disneylandia (ultimately, just Disneyland), and the location shifted south to an orange grove in Anaheim.

Anaheim, which in the early 1950s was predicted to become the population center of Southern California, was selected from among more than 70 proposed sites for Disneyland. Beach towns were the most frequently suggested, but Walt believed it would be impossible to compete against the ocean.

In 1954, in perhaps what turned out to be one of the most fortuitous investments in the history of Southern California real estate, the Fujishige family paid $10,000 for the 56 acres of strawberry fields across from (what would become) Disneyland. In the late 1990s, the Fujishige family sold 52.5 of those 56 acres to Disneyland...
for $99.9 million.

To raise money to build the park, Walt borrowed on his life insurance policy, cashed in on property he owned, and got the American Broadcasting Company (then brand new) to contribute more than $500,000 in exchange for a one-third ownership and a television series. The Disney Company not only bought out ABC's interest two years later, but in 1995, they bought ABC.

Although the 1954 Disneyland TV series begin with animation of fireworks, Disneyland did not have any pyrotechnical displays until mid-1957. The "Fantasy in The Sky" show was the brainchild of the park's entertainment director Tommy Walker in response to Walt's desire to get guests to stay for (and after) dinner.

The most popular (and elaborate) fireworks display — "Remember…Dreams Come True" — was created for Disneyland's 50th anniversary in 2005 and its development was so top secret that designers went all the way to China's Gobi Desert to do the trial run.

One of the best in-park views of the fireworks display — from the second-floor platform of the Main Street train station — also puts guests in a position for the quickest exit.

WHO KNEW

Among the "expert" amusement park advice given Walt while Disneyland was in its early stages of construction was to not waste money on landscaping, design details, or architecture ("particularly a castle") that did not directly generate revenue or was there only for show.

Disneyland is the most Instagram geotagged location in the world.

David Hoffman is an Emmy-award winning producer, writer, and on-air correspondent, and the author of 15 books on all aspects of popular culture. He is not ashamed to admit that he has made the 36.9-mile drive from his home in Los Angeles to Main Street in Disneyland just to get a corn dog.